THE TRUTH ABOUT
RODRIGO BORGIA
POPE ALEXANDER VI

THE TRUTH ABOUT
RODRIGO BORGIA
POPE ALEXANDER VI

N. M. Gwynne M. A. (Oxon.)

TRADIBOOKS

© Copyright Tradibooks 2008

ISBN 978-2-917813-03-4

TRADIBOOKS

Rouchas Sud

47180 Saint-Sauveur de Meilhan, France

http://www.tradibooks.com – *tradibooks@orange.fr*

CONTENTS

FOREWORD

The purpose of this short book is to marshal for the reader sufficient factual evidence to demonstrate beyond the slightest doubt that Rodrigo Borgia, Pope Alexander VI, is one of the most misrepresented men, if not indeed *the* most misrepresented man, in history. Specifically, this study seeks to show that, far from being the monster depicted by some of his biographers, or even merely the pope who combined having the best interests of the Church at heart with leading an outrageously immoral private life, as depicted by others, he was one of the greatest and holiest of all the popes of the last thousand years, and that all the evidence that is reliable and unprejudiced shows his personal conduct to be that of either a saint or a near saint.

I have based this study mainly on a five-volume work called *Material for a History of Pope Alexander VI, His Relatives and His Time*, put together by the Rt. Rev. Msgr. Peter De Roo and published at the end of the nineteenth century. Despite its modest title, this work is an immense feat of research and deduction, and it must be stressed that, although almost unknown and not even referred to by many of Pope Alexander VI's other biographers,[1] it is

---

[1] Perhaps some evidence of the lack of interest shown in the book of researchers is provided by the fact that in 1981 the pages of the British Library copy, from which the present writer extracted much of what follows,

far more complete and scholarly than any other biography despite being purely factual and never polemical.

Compared to Msgr. De Roo's work, the scope of this one is of course extremely limited. Msgr. De Roo derived his information from vast quantities of pontifical and other documents issued during the time of the maligned pope, and it would be impossible in a short space even to attempt a complete summary of what is to be found in his volumes. My purpose is simply to bring to light information and evidence concerning Pope Alexander VI and the scarcely less famous members of his family—for they too have suffered at the hands of the libel-mongers—that are sufficient to expose and completely destroy the false picture and to go some way to painting a true one. Anyone who wishes to go further into the subject must turn to De Roo's work itself, in which all the evidence is superbly set out and full references are given for all documents cited, and with many extracts from them reproduced at length.

Doubtless it will be asked why it should be legitimate to place so much credence on one author flying in the face of the unanimous conclusions of all others who have examined the subject. There are a number of answers.

First, it is not, logically, a valid refutation of De Roo to point out that he is alone in completely rehabilitating Pope Alexander VI. The truth on any given subject depends not in the least on how

---

had not even been cut! This would not be remarkable in a publication of which there was a plentiful supply, but it certainly is surprising in one such as this, which is virtually unobtainable in England and scarcely less so in America.

many people share an opinion about it, but solely on the evidence on which they base their opinion. As Saint Thomas Aquinas succinctly put it, "Do not heed by whom a thing is said, but, rather, what is said."[2]

Indeed, while it certainly does not constitute proof, the fact that a serious and careful historian, which De Roo certainly was, should expend enormous labour in producing a work for, clearly, no financial gain and indeed for little reward in this world other than ridicule, is at least evidence that what he writes should be examined very carefully indeed.

Perhaps this can be best explained by analogy with a key incident in the murder story Whose Body? by best-selling detective-story writer Dorothy L. Sayers. In the story, a junior doctor disagrees with a senior and eminent surgeon whom he is assisting to conduct an autopsy, as to the interval between the victim's injury and the victim's death. Naturally everyone accepts the judgement of the renowned medical authority...except of course, Sayers's sleuth Lord Peter Wimsey, who points out that the junior doctor would only contest the opinion of his widely-respected superior when the truth was so elementary and obvious that he was utterly certain of being right. The conclusion, therefore, is that the senior surgeon is the guilty party. Similarly, if a historian, without any attempt at sensationalism, and potentially at the expense of his credibility, and thus for no possible motive other than love of truth, produces a work which flies in the face of

---

[2] Letter of Saint Thomas Aquinas to Brother John, *De modo studendi* ("On how to study").

all other well-regarded historians, that is even in itself strong circumstantial evidence that there is a strong possibility that popular belief is wrong.

Naturally I do not put forward this first answer to the question posed in the last paragraph as *proof* of Pope Alexander's innocence. I do so only to show that the question was founded on a false premise and that the loneliness of Msgr. De Roo's position is no better evidence that he is wrong than that he is right.

A second and even better answer is that much of what De Roo says is simply self-evident as soon as one reads it, and that, as will be shown in the course of this essay, the generally accepted view of Alexander VI cannot possibly stand up to the examination of anyone who is prepared to consider it systematically and attempt to reconcile all the internal contradictions it contains.

A third answer is that no biographer, even among those who mention De Roo and deny what he says, has ever tried systematically to refute him. On the contrary, brief, bland and sneering dismissals are the means by which his massive feat of scholarship, when it is not completely ignored, is discarded. For example Fr. Thurston S.J. in his *No Popery – Chapters on Anti-Papal Prejudice*, a book written in defence of the papacy—and how much more effectively a man is denigrated by those purporting to be on the same side than by his overt enemies!—wrote (page 10):

> There can be little palliation for the moral depravity and the shameless nepotism of Rodrigo Borgia, who, in spite of a simoniacal election, ruled the Church for eleven years (1492-1503) as Alexander VI, without any serious opposition

being raised against his authority. Attempts have been made—notably of late years by Mgr. Peter De Roo in a work which runs to no less than five volumes—to exculpate the Pontiff from the gross misconduct with which he stands charged. But the whole contention, like that of previous apologists, completely breaks down in the face of documentary evidence leaving no loophole for escape. Burchard's Diary would alone suffice to prove that the dissolute life of Alexander continued after he became Head of the Church, and in the face of the critical edition of the Diary by Celani, it cannot any longer be pretended that the passages reflecting on the Pope's scandalous libertinage are malicious interpolations. Moreover, in the latest edition of von Pastor's *Geschichte der Päpste* fresh evidence of irregularities is adduced confirming his previous judgment. The only excuse that can be offered—and it is a poor excuse enough—is that under the neo-paganism of the Renaissance public opinion condoned every kind of moral laxity. Alexander, says Señor Sanchis y Sivera, 'lived in a state of society in which illegitimate children were not held in less consideration than legitimate offspring,' and he goes on to quote the saying of Aeneas Silvius (Pope Pius II), 'Italy is governed by people born out of wedlock.'

It would be easy to multiply testimonies to the same effect from many other sources. Alexander VI was not the only Pope of the Renaissance period against whom grave charges were made, but there is hardly any other who, upon reliable evidence, stands convicted of shameless concubinage during his actual tenure of the papacy.

Thus is dismissed years of painstaking research and a vast quantity of carefully assessed and documented evidence without the labour that would have been involved in refuting so much as a single one of the arguments put forward by Msgr. De Roo.

And a fourth answer to the question is that the biographers whom Msgr. De Roo contradicts are *not* unanimous. Indeed there are almost as many different pen-portraits of Pope Alexander VI as there are people who have written about him with any seriousness, and almost the only thing that they are agreed upon is that he led to *some* extent a private life which would have been grossly scandalous in a simple priest, let alone in a pope. In general, in other words, they contradict each other scarcely less than the conclusions of each of them contradict those of De Roo, so that De Roo certainly is not a one-man minority against a single picture painted consistently by all the rest.

Right from the outset of any attempt to assess Pope Alexander VI, therefore, a researcher cannot avoid the task of assessing who is Alexander's most reliable biographer out of many who differ among themselves very considerably; and what can be said about Msgr. De Roo is that he has taken the trouble to research the *primary* sources, which the others have not.

Although for some things Msgr. De Roo is the only authority that can be cited, because on these things he is the only authority who has taken the trouble to unearth and derive the unavoidable conclusion from the information, he is not the only author that I use in this essay. Some of the libels against poor Alexander are so glaringly obvious as being libels that other authors have been unable to avoid noticing that they can have no foundation in fact even without checking original documents; and although Msgr. De Roo refutes these satisfactorily by himself, I believe that readers may be, even if they should not be, happier if they see some of his conclusions corroborated by other authors. I shall make special use of a book called *The Borgia Pope—Alexander the Sixth* by Orestes Ferrara, published by Sheed and Ward in 1942. It is quite valuable for our purposes because it is evident that Ferrara is not prejudiced in favour of Alexander VI, indeed he accepts many of the allegations against his subject. At the same time, he is fully aware that the more extravagant of the allegations are without foundation, and, in addition, he fills a gap left by De Roo in that he provides some valuable insights into how and why the legend was originally built up.

I conclude this foreword by mentioning that I do not discourage any reader who considers that he has a critical eye that is reasonably accurate, to look through works quite definitely hostile to Alexander VI as part of any further research he may wish to do. As I have already indicated, in most of them he will find internal contradictions which simply in themselves are revealing. He will also find facts which, if he thinks about them carefully, seem hopelessly out of place if the legend be true—examples of which are Alexander VI's generally acknowledged popularity; his eating habits, which were so ascetic as to have been widely remarked upon by his contemporaries; and the astonishing absence of information that exists about his allegedly grossly immoral private life before he became pope but while nevertheless still a very prominent public figure. In my submission, while it would not be possible to obtain the true picture of Pope Alexander VI without the material provided by Msgr. De Roo, a reader has only to *look* at a fair cross-section of other biographies, rather than gaze at them in a stupor, to realize that there is much about the legend, in any of its versions, that simply does not add up.

INTRODUCTION

Alexander VI is variously depicted as being: dissolute, licentious, and even, by perhaps the majority of authors, totally depraved. The following is a summary of the main allegations against him:

- that he had many concubines;
- that he fathered, and acknowledged his paternity of, several illegitimate children, including Cesar and Lucretia Borgia;
- that he committed incest with Lucretia Borgia, the daughter of one of his concubines;
- that he was a murderer (having, for instance, stabbed a twelve year old boy to death);
- that he was a gambler and debauchee;
- that he contracted venereal disease;
- that he committed suicide;
- that he practiced simony on a vast scale;
- that he profited hugely, and many of his relatives also, from his Papal office; and
- that he made extensive use of deceit, murder and robbery for the purposes of filling the papal coffers.

To add some flesh to the skeleton just given, I quote from *The Borgia Pope—Alexander the Sixth* (p.1):

For public life, the word Borgia calls up a vision of poison and dagger, of malevolent cunning, incest, fratricide, perfidy unlimited; and for the Church, simony, nepotism, utter want of belief, something very close to atheism. In common opinion, the comparatively short period in which Pope Alexander occupied the throne of Peter was a time of abomination so immeasurable that other ages, no matter how notorious their infamy, can only approach and never equal it. The example he set incited the basest men of the lowest passions to employ the worst means to attain their perverted ends. If Machiavelli is the theorist of methods repudiated by the human conscience, the Borgias represent the full practice of precisely those methods.

According to the legend one Rodrigo Llanzol, a kind of soldier, a cross between a bandit and a gentleman, vicious and violent, one day changed his second name to Borgia and entered the Church at the instance of his uncle, Pope Calixtus III, who proceeded to confer the purple upon him against the will of the Sacred College.

The new Cardinal led a debauched life, in which lust and greed for money strove for first place. Emboldened by continuing success, he bought the conclave on the death of Innocent VIII and made himself pope. Under the name of Alexander VI he murdered many of his former colleagues in the consistory, and others besides, using a poison called *cantarella*; he involved his son Cesar in the most sordid adventures; and like Cesar committed incest—and with the same woman, his daughter, the unspeakable Lucretia. He seized the money of all his victims. He never kept his word. A great hypocrite, he was a secret accessory in the murders attributed to his son, whom he continued to love and raise to the highest honours, though he knew perfectly well that that base man had had another of his children, the Duke of Gandia, murdered. He destroyed the peace of Europe, invited the barbarians to the conquest of Italy, stole the Church's temporal goods for the enrichment of Cesar, and robbed many princes of their towns, their castles, and their houses. In the end he died a victim of his own poison, just when under the thrust of his cupidity he was preparing the destruction by this same poison of a Cardinal and other dignitaries of the Church. As everybody was in terror of him and no one could be sure of seeing the next day dawn as long as he lived, his death was a glorious relief for Rome and all Europe.

There you have in its main lines, the story of the Borgias, as it has come down to us. You will find it in history books, in popular tradition, in melodrama, in fiction.

All the allegations are untrue. Even though Orestes Ferrara does not acknowledge that the myth is as completely without foundation as this essay is intended to demonstrate—he cannot accept, for instance, that Alexander VI had no children—his next few words are entirely appropriate:

> Yet it is quite certain that the palpitating story that now occupies the general mind is a sheer invention. What passes for the history of the Borgias is a legend, in part invented by contemporaries and added to by later authors; a legend which, like all legends, has taken shape gradually. To make it plausible it has been necessary little by little to add imaginary acts to real acts, then to alter proportions, turn guesses into realities, and finally, with the aid of distance, transform the whole thing into a piece of drama; the history of Alexander VI as it has reached us is a tissue of inaccuracies, extraordinarily easy to disprove the moment recourse is had to contemporary documents in a spirit of sane criticism.

Accusation after accusation collapses, not only for want of proof, but still more because it was evidently impossible for him to have committed the crime in question.

The true facts can be summarized as follows:

He laboured hard in his capacity as head of the Church; he worked to preserve intact, and to propagate, divine doctrine; he made strenuous efforts to reform the clergy and the laity; he was zealous to promote piety; and he toiled patiently and continuously and made great sacrifices to save Christian Europe from the destructive incursions of the cruel Turks. Furthermore he had, as will be shown, the gravest reasons to act as strongly as he did towards the kings of France and Naples. In his dealings with the vassals of the Church he first tried munificence and mercy, and when this failed, his conduct was directed by justice and duty. He was a man of good moral character and conspicuous piety and an excellent Pope.

The foregoing quotation corresponds to the picture of Alexander VI painted by Msgr. De Roo in volume 1 of his work. Let us turn once more to Ferrara for a rather more detailed summary, which, however, concentrating on him in his capacity as a public figure, makes no reference to his personal sanctity:

In fact as we come to see the truth, we begin to realize that in the whole Renaissance period there was no man who had a loftier idea of the liberty of the Church, of States and of individuals; no man who had a truer appreciation of the evil to be feared from the powers of the period which aimed at hegemony; no man who used more strength and skill than he in the effort to preserve Italy from the disaster of foreign domination. Alexander was a jovial, far-sighted, moderate man, well-balanced in mind and body. Having lived nearly half a century in Rome, and having been for almost the whole of his life part of the ecclesiastical organization, he had come to a profound respect for all the interests of the Catholic Church, a respect greater than for his own life. He was prepared to compromise upon all purely human questions, but inflexible upon whatever concerned the rights of religion. He was the type of "political priest", cautious and slow to act in the fact of the unforeseen, but brave to the point of heroism in defence of the great Institution whose direction had been entrusted to him.

Thoroughly versed in the politics of his day and the needs of the Church, he tried to prevent evils which were to afflict Italy for four centuries after. If his policy of international balance had remained that of the Vatican, if Julius II had not destroyed it by his temper and his utterly chaotic mind, the Church and Italy would have been spared much suffering.

He succeeded in doing more for other countries indeed than for Italy. In Spain he helped most effectively towards national unity; and in the Americas he fixed the line of demarcation for the possession of newly discovered lands. In the purely ecclesiastical domain, he drew up a program of religious reform not vastly improved upon either by the Reformation or the Counter-Reformation. He was the great precursor of the Council of Trent. With paternal indulgence, he pardoned the twofold treason of certain Cardinals, towards the States of the Church and towards himself. He never showed the harshness and cruelty normal at the time, save when it was a question of delivering Rome from the factious tyranny of the great nobles, a truly sordid crew. He was no mystic and no saint.[3] He had the merits and the

---

[3] The statements that he was no mystic and no saint and (stated later in the paragraph) a lover of pleasure are far from being definitely true, and there is good evidence, which will be cited in this study, that the last of them is definitely untrue.

faults of a man of action aiming at success.[4] He was a Pope, and a great Pope, of the Renaissance. He was a nepotist and a temporal prince, a lover of work, a lover of pleasure, inflexible upon the interests of religion, a legalist in public affairs.

Thus there is a huge contrast between the reality and the legend. And the contrast cannot fail to trouble the mind of every reader and every writer. It troubled my own mind. It is to this that we owe the kind of uncertainty to be found in many modern historians, who when they come to speak of the Borgias deny and affirm the same facts, and are guilty of incredibly contradictory judgements.

And I hope the contrast between reality and the legend will trouble the minds of the readers of this little book also. It is my contention that appreciation of Pope Alexander VI among Catholics in general, as opposed to merely a minority of dedicated seekers after the truth, is long overdue; and that it is grounds for sorrow that the cause for his beatification has never been opened. Those who think that I exaggerate, please read on.

---

[4] Again as will emerge during the course of this essay, the assertion that he had "the faults of a man or action aiming at success" is far from being certainly true. Indeed, it is gratuitous to assume that a man of action aiming at success must necessarily have faults. To cite but a few examples of people of action aiming at success who had fewer faults than most, I draw attention to Our Lord Himself, who of course had none, St. Paul, King Alfred the Great, King St. Louis IX of France, St. Francis of Assisi, St. Dominic, and St. Joan of Arc.

CHAPTER 1

ALEXANDER VI'S LIFE AND
ACHIEVEMENTS

Rodrigo Borgia (later Pope Alexander VI) was born on the last day of 1431 or the first day of 1432. He left Spain and arrived in Italy in 1449, leaving school having graduated not simply as Doctor of Law but as "the most eminent and judicious jurisprudent." He was created Cardinal in 1456. Every Cardinal in Rome and two others outside Rome were in favour of this creation and there was no opposition to it whatever. (Vol. II)[5]

No fewer than five popes under whom he served competed among themselves as to who should honour him most. (Vol. I)

In 1492, at the age of 60, he was unanimously elected pope. He died on 18th August, 1503.

The following is a précis of Alexander VI's qualities as outlined by De Roo:

He was extremely good looking, cheerful, used "refined and sweet language," and was graceful. Not one contemporary author alleges that he ever once passed time in female

---

[5] Volume numbers cited here and subsequently refer to the volume in Msgr. De Roo's *Material for a History of Pope Alexander VI* from which the information just given is directly taken.

company—even the dubious and possibly spurious letter of Pius II only suggests that he was indulging in recreation not far from a company of Sienese ladies who were dancing. He had a vast intellect, great charm, a vigorous and penetrating mind, good judgement, an excellent memory and much knowledge. Jason Mayno: "Thou goest ahead with inflexible rectitude, unbiased judgement, incorruptible integrity." He was cheerful and gifted with a restful disposition. He was also a natural orator, a pleasant conversationalist, an expert in Canon Law and Theology, and "so familiar with Holy Writ that his speeches sparkled with well chosen texts from Sacred Scripture." He never ceased to be a student: if not occupied by Divine service or Church affairs he would be reading books. He also wrote for the instruction of others. (Vol. II)

It is admitted even by his enemies that he was a protector and promoter of literature and the sciences.

He was a model of piety in his worship of the Blessed Sacrament and in his veneration of the Holy Virgin and the Saints. (Vol. III) His piety, especially towards the Blessed Sacrament, was so remarkable that even his enemies remarked on it (though naturally this piety was sometimes attributed by them to hypocrisy). Sixtus IV said that Rodrigo's love for the Virgin Mary was no less fervent than his own.

He was loved by all who knew him: by the popes, cardinals, officials of the Roman Court, and by the common people of his city. He was very generous and charitable towards the poor and the sick. (Vol. II)

Contrary to all allegations, Alexander VI scrupulously observed all existing laws that governed matrimonial cases.

To supplement these generalities, let us take a closer look at some of Alexander's particular undertakings and achievements, still using Msgr. De Roo as our source:

Alexander VI started reforms of the Church in Rome, Ireland, Germany, France, Spain, England, Portugal and Italy. De Roo goes into considerable detail concerning what he accomplished and attempted to accomplish in each country. He also wanted general reform. He prepared a Bull for this purpose, which was however never published because he discovered that a Bull would not be sufficient and that a general Synod would be needed instead. Hence, eventually, the Council of Trent, of which he can justly be regarded as the original inspiration.

Constant disturbances and wars in Italy and attacks by the Turks on Christian provinces prevented the opportunity of a venerable and peaceful assembly. He was therefore only able to make particular corrections and to promote moral improvements, both of which he did.

In the Vatican there are preserved the records of hundreds of Bulls and briefs of Alexander VI, which abolish abuses at the Roman Court, correct and reform religious communities of both sexes (not only in Italy but in every province in Christendom), and encourage all who endeavour to promote the holy life. Old Vatican documents clearly show that he was taking great pains to bring about a universal reform which not many years later was worked out by the Council of Trent. (Vol. III)

He was also responsible for a considerable spreading of the Faith: in particular in Greenland, in the Congo, Granada, the newly discovered West Indies, and in Spanish and Portuguese overseas possessions.

He did not, as is alleged and generally assumed, grant one half of the New World to Spain and the other half to Portugal. All he did was to confirm the existing arrangements which Spain and Portugal would not have regarded as binding unless confirmed by the pope. This was the custom in those days. A Bull used for such a purpose was rather like a modern patent protecting the inventor or discoverer. (Vol. III)

Alexander VI was the originator, at least in part, of the devout custom of saying the Angelus at the ringing of a bell three times a day. He instigated this in order to invoke Our Lady for help against the Turks. The custom had partly existed in earlier times but previous similar ordinances had lapsed. Following his recommendation of it, the custom of saying the Angelus soon spread throughout Italy and at the beginning of the 16th Century was universally observed in France. It then spread to all countries in the world. (Vol. III)

Alexander VI was responsible for an enormous promotion of learning, including the rebuilding of the Roman University and the establishment and favouring of several other universities. He restored several churches, improved the Vatican Palace, and rebuilt the castle of Sant'Angelo. He improved the streets and aqueducts of Rome and repaired all the city walls, gates and several bridges. He also restored the fountains of Rome. (Vol. IV)

In his attitude to the rebellions against him, a great, if not the principal, motive of Alexander's efforts to restore the papal authority in the Pontifical States proceeded from his inborn love for the masses of the people, who gave him in return their unfaltering loyalty and affection from the beginning of his cardinalate to the end of his life. He was fully aware that in many cities his subjects were being corrupted by the evil examples of their Lords; he saw them despoiled and robbed by noble as well as ignoble brigands and highwaymen; and he saw their castles stolen and their homes destroyed by rival factions of the local nobility or by petty tyrants who were at war with one another when not at war with the pope himself.

He was therefore fully justified in drawing the sword, not only to secure his personal rights, but also to secure the peace and happiness of his people with whose welfare he was especially concerned. While his foreign policies were directed by the strictest justice, his management of internal affairs and of his arts of administration had for their object the benefit and great good of his subjects. (Vol. III)

Among his achievements was his successful fight to prevent the Mohammedan Turks from acquiring more European territory. The Turks assaulted, for instance, Hungary, territory in Albania belonging to Venice, Dalmatia, Istria, Corfu and Poland. He united all Europe against the Turks, and a treaty to which he formally assented lasted several years. (Vol. V)

One can summarize by saying that Alexander's acts performed while Supreme Pontiff were so astonishing in their number and importance that his life cannot possibly have been one of ease and self-gratification. (Vol. V)

CHAPTER 2

ALEXANDER VI'S "CONCUBINES"

There is no document or credible contemporary witness to suggest that Alexander VI ever spoke to, or even saw, either the Spanish Vanozza (the wife of his nephew, William Raymond Lanzol y de Borgia, and mother of their five children which are alleged to be the children of Alexander) or the Roman Vanozza (who is supposed to have borne him seven children). Both are alleged by various authorities to have been his concubines (Vol. II), but De Roo reports that there is no specific information in the writings of any of the contemporaries of Alexander VI, or of any subsequent historian of either young Rodrigo or Cardinal Borgia, of Pope Alexander VI's having ever on any actual occasion been seen in the company of the Spanish Vanozza, with whom he is most persistently linked, or of his having spoken to her, met her, or even looked at her.

Even Gregorovius and Pastor (the former minutely describes the furniture of her residence and her features) know of no such incident. They and the other enemies of the slandered pope "vent their hatred for him in gross but unproved and unprovable generalities." (Vol. II)

Anonymous pamphlets, in addition to accusing him of stabbing a 12 year old boy to death (a crime that the law courts nevertheless saw fit to ignore) and of being a compulsive gambler, claimed that he had a mistress, was a debaucher and had committed incest with his daughter by his mistress. Despite these accusations, *no* contemporary writer of any name suggests that Rodrigo either as a youth, as cardinal or as pope, committed *any* unbecoming deed whatsoever.

There *is* extant a rebuke addressed to him by Pius II dated 11th June 1560 which accuses him, when aged twenty-nine, of a single instance of public laxity in moral principles—specifically of dancing without restraint. If the document is genuine, and De Roo tends to think it is, it contains no proof of the accusation and specifically states that it is based on hearsay. De Roo points out that the letter was written within twenty four hours of the alleged scandal, so that there was no time for the Pope to give critical consideration to what he had heard at third or fourth hand. He also notes that ladies did not dance *lasciviously* in those days.

Rodrigo replied to the letter disproving the accusation, and exposing the exaggerations and misrepresentations in the accusation, and claiming that his behaviour had been guiltless and blameless. The Pope then acknowledged that he had been deceived but held that Rodrigo could not be entirely without culpability. De Roo believes this latter statement must have been face-saving and supports this view by the fact that Pius II continued without interruption to grant Rodrigo favours.

De Roo also asks pertinently why, at the same time as these accusations were being made, Pius II did not mention his "scandalous affair with the Roman courtesan, Zanozia (or Vanozza) Catanei, who bore him seven Borgia children," and indeed why none of the three successors to Pius II noticed his alleged infamies if this relatively small indiscretion caused so much fuss? (Vol. II)

Why indeed?

He has been further accused of having twenty-five women in the Vatican every evening, of assaulting a married woman, and of keeping a harem. It is sufficient to say that there is *no* mention of *any* of these crimes or scandals in contemporary despatches.

He has been accused of concubinage with the noble Lady Julia Farnese and it has been said that Laura Orsini was his child by Lady Julia. This would be surprising as Laura Orsini married Nicholas della Rovere, a nephew of Pope Julius II (Alexander's successor) who was a bitter enemy of his predecessor and detested everything to do with the Borgias. It seems unlikely, to say the least, that Alexander VI's bitter enemy would have tolerated Alexander's illegitimate daughter becoming the wife of his favoured nephew. (Vol. V)

CHAPTER 3

ALEXANDER VI'S "CHILDREN"

The family tree is as follows:

The eldest sister of Alexander VI was Donna Juana (or Joanna) de Borja[6] (who was born in 1425). She was married to Pedro Guillen de Romani. She had a younger son, Jotre Lanzol y Borgia (who was therefore the nephew of Alexander VI). Her eldest son was William Raymond[7] Lanzol y de Borgia, (also, of course, the nephew of Alexander VI).

The William Raymond who was the eldest son of Donna Juana and the nephew of Alexander VI, married Violanta (or Vanotia)—the Spanish Vanozza.

Many records about William Raymond have been suppressed. He died in 1481, leaving a wife with a large family of children. On his death, Cardinal Rodrigo (the future Pope Alexander VI), who up to the day of his death befriended all unfortunates, took pity on his nephew's orphans and became a second father to them. This charity cost him dearly; but it should be noted that no writer before

---

[6] *Borja* is the Spanish spelling of *Borgia*.

[7] William Raymond's brother, Jofre, also had a son called William Raymond—this William Raymond was therefore the nephew of William Raymond, eldest son of Donna Juana, and thus great-nephew of Alexander VI.

1481, nor indeed at any time before the death of Alexander VI, either accused Rodrigo of any act of immorality, or of having a concubine, or of being familiar or unreserved with any woman. Nor was any suspicion of such behaviour even voiced. Nevertheless, on the occasion of the second marriage of Vanozza Borgia de Cathaneis, the future Pontiff apparently suddenly acquired a whole family of children of whom no contemporary document formally names him the father. De Roo says that there are many forged documents surrounding this aspect of the life of Alexander VI and indeed many other aspects. (Vol. I)

One source says: "When Rodrigo came to Rome, he lived for a long time with a Spanish widow who had apparently two daughters with whom he also misbehaved." And the same source adds that the liaison was apparently so openly accepted that the widow even took his name. The truth is that Vanozza signed her name Borgia with very good reason! She was, after all, the widow of William Raymond Borgia, nephew of Alexander VI. There is absolute silence about Vanozza's earlier years when she was having her children; and one might reasonably ask why she was not the subject or target of contemporary satirists or poets or letter-writers. There is absolutely no record that she ever visited the apostolic palace, or even so much as met or wrote to Alexander VI. The true fact is that after William Raymond's death she married again and sent her three youngest children to Rome to be cared for by Cardinal Rodrigo while she remained in Spain. She placed the three children in the care of their elderly cousin Adriana del Mila. Vanozza had no children by her second husband. Eventually she moved to Rome and died in 1518 having led a quiet and retiring life. (Vol. I)

The sons of William Raymond were as follows: Pierluigi, Giovanni, Cesar, Jofre. His daughter was Lucretia. The original documents have been so tampered with that the only evidence which establishes that these five children were his children is indirect evidence. There is, however, a considerable amount of such indirect evidence. (Vol. I)

Neither Cesar nor Lucretia was heard of in Italy until 1488.

All of William Raymond's children were born in Spain while Alexander VI was in Rome. There is, therefore, no possibility of their being his offspring. Contemporary evidence shows that Vanozza Cathanei de Borgia was the mother of the children but *not one historian of that time* asserts that Alexander VI was their father or had any kind of relations with their mother. Even Savonarola, who accuses him of several vices, does not assert this.

Alexander VI frequently used the expression "sons" and "daughters" in correspondence; and it was sometimes applied to the children of William Raymond de Borgia, his nephews and nieces. He did indeed address Lucretia, in a letter, as his "dearest daughter". He also, however, addressed Queen Isabella of Spain as "our beloved daughter", while no family relationship has been alleged to have existed between *them*! His actual words to Lucretia were "our dearest daughter in Christ". (Vol. I)

Also, while Alexander VI called Giovanni and Cesar "his favourite sons", he uses the same words to address the Emperor Maximilian, his envoy Marrobald and all male Christians with whom he had any correspondence! It is also noteworthy that Cesar never called the Pope his beloved father. (Vol. I) According to De Roo, it was also quite natural that the common people should have referred to the orphans of his dead nephew as his children when they saw him, in his capacity of cardinal and pope, taking a fatherly care of them, promoting their education and advancement and receiving them at the pontifical palace; but no disgrace was attached to this relationship, as is demonstrated by the constant devotion and attachment of the common people to Alexander VI. (Vol. I)

Everything changed on the death of Alexander VI, when "the tempest of hatred of the nobility broke loose against him." The popular terms of *son* and *daughter* were generally changed into *illegitimate son* or *illegitimate daughter*, or into *bastard*, by the malcontents of his reform administration, by the salaried scribblers of princes whom he had justly punished, and by the diarists and historians of the following period, whose slanders went unpunished, if not encouraged, during the reign of "an unfriendly successor".

During his lifetime, however, no fewer than five consecutive popes under whom he served as cardinal, instead of shamefully deposing him for the crime of being the sacrilegious father of several children, had competed among themselves as to who should honour him most. It should also be noted that several contemporaries described the children as nephews and nieces, a description which also appeared in some official and business documents. (Vol. I)

CHAPTER 4

SOME OTHER ACCUSATIONS

Alexander VI is accused of deceit and of robbery, and of murder for the purposes of filling the papal treasury. However, the sole source of the accusation that he murdered Cardinal Michiel was a man who himself was a murderer and was condemned to death. No one at the time believed the accuser. (Vol. V)

As already mentioned, anonymous pamphlets accused Alexander of stabbing a twelve year old boy to death, a crime that was nevertheless ignored by the law courts. It is worth emphasizing once more: no contemporary writer of any name alleged in Rodrigo Borgia any unbecoming deed whatever, whether as youth, cardinal or pope. (Vol. II)

On the death of Pius II, Rodrigo was unable to crown his successor Paul II because he was at the time suffering from the plague. Although no contemporary says so, von Pastor alleged that Rodrigo Borgia was unable to perform at this event because he was suffering from venereal disease. (Vol. III)

The final accusation against Alexander VI was that he committed suicide. This De Roo satisfactorily refutes. He also gives the particular circumstances of his sickness and exemplary death. He died naturally of fever on 18th August, 1503. (Vol. V)

CHAPTER 5

ALEXANDER VI'S FINANCES AND THE ACCUSATION OF SIMONY

De Roo sheds much light on the topic of the attribution of benefices. No candidate could receive Holy Orders unless he possessed one or more ecclesiastical benefices whose revenues were sufficient to procure for him an honest subsistence, unless he should have vowed voluntary poverty in some religious order. Benefices were the ordinary, indeed the only, real resources for keeping up the temples of the Almighty, the houses of charity, the popular schools, the clergy and all people who served these aspects of Christian civilization. Charitable and rich people, both lay and priests, who were interested in the welfare and education of young clergymen, had provided benefices to be applied, in the manner which the givers had intended, by bishops or popes. It should be realized that the benefices were never adequate and in the 15th century the popes were the poorest of all the clergy. The greater the responsibility and the higher the position of officers at the papal court, the more and bigger benefices were needed by them to cover the expenses needed for intercourse with kings and princes. (Vol. II)

As far as the administration of the finances of the Church is concerned, Alexander during his pontificate was exceptionally prudent. I quote from *The Borgias* by Michael Mallet, an author who cannot be thought biased in Alexander VI's favour since he supports a large number of the allegations commonly made against him.

> As we shall see, he succeeded in balancing the budget of the Church for the first time for half a century, and there is evidence that the provincial treasuries of the Papal States were more efficiently run under his supervision than they had been for a long time.
>
> Panvinio says that as a private individual Alexander lived always poorly, and that both his sleep and meals were very short; but he was stately and grand as soon as he appeared in his Cardinal's hat. This is because he believed that, for the edification of the people, it was the duty of every clergyman to appear becomingly before the public, according to his rank and condition. Despite the fact that all hostile authors assert that he was a very rich Cardinal, he had no real estate except for his residence. This was too small for his accommodation and he had to rent other adjoining buildings. De Roo shows (with tables) his expenses and income to have been about equal and states that more than once he was on the verge of financial ruin. (Vol. II)[8]

His personal expenditure, far from being lavish and indulgent, was negligible. He spent very little on meals, only having one dish at mealtimes. His table was so frugally furnished that Cesar de Borgia and some of the Cardinals avoided all invitations to dine with him. In the account books of the Roman Archives of State, there are items for wine used by Julius II; but for Alexander VI the

---

[8] Michael Mallet, *The Borgias*, Paladin, St. Albans, 1969 (p. 198).

expenses for beverage were so insignificant that no mention is found anywhere.

He did, however, spend large sums on building, and on wars against rebellious lords, and on almsdeeds. (Vol. V) For further confirmation of the asceticism of Alexander VI's eating habits and the modesty of his personal expenditure, I turn again to the author, generally speaking hostile to him, whom I quoted earlier in the chapter, Michael Mallet. After, early in his book (p.16) saying, "His court, *despite certain surprising ascetic features*,[9] was that of a Renaissance prince," Mallet goes into more detail on page 204:

> A very different picture[10] is revealed by a study of household accounts of his pontificate. The Ferrarese ambassador, Boccaccio, reported that usually only one course was served at the papal table and that Cardinals used to avoid eating with the Pope because they fared so poorly in his company. This frugality is amply borne out by the household expenses. Alexander spent approximately 20,000 ducats a year on his household which was very similar to the expenses of his uncle, Calixtus III, whose frugality and parsimony were notorious. This was at a time when the size of the papal household was steadily rising; only a few years later Leo X was able to spend up to 100,000 [ducats] a year. These expenses covered the salaries of his immediate household, which numbered about sixty, and the living costs of a rather larger group who lived and worked in the Vatican; in addition, there were incidental expenses with the Vatican and almsgiving.

---

[9] My emphasis.

[10] That is, a very different picture from what Mallet alleges to be Alexander's extravagance in pursuit of the temporal aims of the Church and the dynastic advancement of his family.

Far from *profiting* by his offices, Alexander VI mortgaged his palace to help pay for an expedition against Turkey, and procured and perfectly equipped and armed a galley for the fleet. As a result he got into deep financial difficulties. (Vol. II)

With regard to his integrity in financial matters, here is a commendation, in stark contrast to the reputation that Alexander "enjoys" today, from one whose experience of his financial dealings would have been most direct. Pope Sixtus IV, in a Bull about the financial settlement of Rodrigo Borgia's account as legate to Spain, wrote, "Your irreproachable virtue demands, and your tried honesty in matters entrusted to you wholly deserves, that we should dutifully attend to your indemnification."

Did Rodrigo Borgia, nevertheless, buy his election to the papacy, as is almost universally alleged? A very material piece of evidence not only against this, but also in favour of Alexander VI in general, is that his election was *unanimous*. As Msgr. De Roo points out, it is simply not credible that *all* the Cardinals went to the conclave as to a market place to meet a buyer rich enough to buy them off. Summarizing what De Roo says on the subject:

At the time of his election, twenty-three Cardinals went into the Sistine Chapel. (Four Cardinals were absent from the election). He received twenty-two votes (obviously he could not vote for himself). This indicates the strongest approval and the highest praise of his former life from the men with whom he had lived so long.

The exceptional unanimity of the election was soon known and referred to all over Christendom. Indeed most, though not all, historians hostile to Alexander acknowledge this. (Vol. II)

His election was welcomed with unprecedented enthusiasm. Sumptuous feasts and rejoicings were held everywhere.

Leaving aside the fact that he did not possess a fraction of the wealth necessary for such an exercise, universal corruption on a scale which would have led every cardinal to vote for him for unworthy motives was simply not possible. Certainly, there were criminal priests and scandalous writers; but there were also at the time thousands of people, both among the clergy and the laity, leading lives of great virtue. Furthermore, there were during the 15th Century more saints, especially in Italy, than in any subsequent century. And, many of the cardinals are admitted to have been exemplary and saintly men (which is why Pastor is forced to deny the unanimity of the election and to reduce the number of electors of Alexander VI to fifteen, which was the required majority): it is clearly not credible that saintly men and corrupt men would all have voted in favour of the same man.

As further proof that there was no question of simony, even supposing he had the money to organise it, some of the historians most hostile to him do not mention it, which they would hardly have failed to do, and there was no contemporary suggestion or suspicion of it. For two and half years no single conclavist set forth the accusation of simony until Cardinal Giuliano della Rovere and Cardinal Asconio Sforza, who were "worse than angry with the Pope," are said to have wanted the King of France, triumphant in Rome, to depose him—alleging that he had bought his holy dignity. From that time on, there was peace and silence about his election until the end of his reign. After his death, his enemies relaunched the accusations, but no proof whatever of simony was ever offered.

Not only was there no question of simony, but it is indeed a well established fact that Alexander VI prosecuted all whom he knew to be guilty of simony. (Vol. V)

CHAPTER 6

NEPOTISM

Nepotism is one of the crimes and scandals of which he and other popes of that time were most frequently accused. It was in fact practiced by Calixtus III, Pius II, Sixtus IV, Innocent VIII, Pius III and Julius II. (Vol. V)

The truth about nepotism in that era is that it was a common and necessary means of protection against the treachery which was epidemic among Italian noblemen. Alexander VI, in fact, at first neglected the Borgia house and favoured the Roman nobility, but found in due course that he had to change his policy. He made three Borgias captains of the Palatine Guard (these were Rodrigo, Raymond and another Rodrigo); he made Aloysius Borgia Vice-Castellan of Tivoli; he made Giovanni Lanzol a foreman of his stables; and he made five Borgias (two Giovannis, Cesar, Francesco, Pierluigi) Cardinals of the Church. Although Pastor says that Julius II did away with the system of nepotism, the facts are that he (Julius II) gave positions to ten members of his family, four of whom he made Cardinals. Alexander VI was therefore following a custom tolerated and approved at the time and practised by both his predecessors and successors. He, however, was criticised more severely for it than was any other pontiff. As already mentioned, he started off by neglecting the Borgias, bestowing castles, territories, etc., on the nobility of the Pontifical States; but all the recipients of his generosity proved to be disloyal or rebellious. To the people in their care they were haughty, corruptive and abusive tyrants, while to his throne they were a menace and a disgrace. He found that to increase their power was to ruin his authority and to augment the misery of his subjects. (Vol. V)

CHAPTER 7

SAVONAROLA

When his supreme authority was attacked by the disobedient monk Savonarola, who was aided by the Florentine republic, Alexander VI punished him—but only after exercising long patience.

Savonarola rebelled against ecclesiastical supremacy, insulted the pope, vilified the clergy, deceived the faithful and tried (and in Florence was partly successful in his attempt) to cause local and universal schism in the Church. In order to raise his credibility, he tried to perform a number of miracles and he made prophecies which did not come true.

There is not even any Protestant who has more violently slandered the Catholic clergy, in particular the Roman clergy, than he. In addition, Savonarola uttered more than one heretical error afterwards to be held, for instance, by Protestantism (notably in the form popularised by John Huss). An example of such error was his assertion that the pope could not validly forbid a preacher to announce the word of God. All Savonarola's writings were expurgated by a Commission of the Council of Trent. Fifteen of his sermons were placed on the Index of Forbidden Books. Saint Ignatius of Loyola would not allow any of his writings to be kept or read in the houses of the Society of Jesus. (Vol. III)

Savonarola was admitted by all his contemporaries to be intelligent, sagacious and learned; he was therefore not an innocent. He was declared to be a cunning deceiver by his own brethren of San Mario; and, as will be shown, he himself confessed his deceit. Contrary to what is often said, Benedict XIV did *not* name him as worthy of canonisation. Savonarola did justly hate the example of immorality set before the Florentines by the ruling de Medici family. However, if there was any sincerity in the origins of his words and actions, he was very swiftly carried into excess. Although he had grievously deceived as an ecclesiastic, it was not as an ecclesiastic that he was hanged and burnt, but as a defeated politician. Savonarola was a politician, and he was condemned on political grounds. He was the victim of the vengeance of other politicians. (Vol. III)

Savonarola was condemned by his own last acts when, freed from pride and mundane interest, he reconciled himself with his Supreme Judge, made a profession of true faith asking pardon of all whom he had injured, accepted a papal indulgence and died a repentant Catholic. He therefore himself confessed his own deceit. (Vol. III)

CHAPTER 8

ALEXANDER VI'S CONTEMPORARY
REPUTATION

Contemporary writers who discussed Alexander include Niccolo Machiavelli (who, remarkably, does not describe Alexander VI as unchaste), de Volterra, Infessura, and Panvinio. There is a complete panegyric, which is contemporary, by Alexis Celadenus, Bishop of Gallipoli. Celadenus makes no attempt whatever to refute or palliate Alexander VI's allegedly immoral life and does not even hint at such an allegation. This is clear evidence that there were at the time no allegations of immorality in connection with Alexander. Another contemporary writer is Michael Fernus. He notes that Alexander VI's natural talents and virtuous life almost *compelled* his colleagues to give him their vote for the papal office. Of immorality and the other depravities which were afterwards imputed to Alexander VI, he writes no word.

Alexander VI *was*, of course, denounced by others. The denunciation by Panvinio described him as a man of inhuman fierceness; of immense avarice and rapacity; of an insatiable desire of procuring, by right or by wrong, dominion for his sons; and as a man who abandoned himself to all sorts of enjoyments whenever he was not pressed by matters of importance. (Vol. II)

Gaspar of Verona said:

It is easier not to speak of this Pope than to say anything calmly of him. His vices were extreme, his virtues were mediocre or, to speak more correctly, were nil. He obtained by evil means the pontifical dignity and retained it by measures no better. I have, so far, not found a single writer who praises him, not one of that time, not one of later years.

The last sentence of this quotation is an outright lie. Alexander VI had been eulogized by Jason Mayno, Jerome Porcius (1493), in various poems and in praises bestowed by the Bishop of Gallipoli in a sermon on 16th September, 1503, to the Sacred College of Cardinals when they were due to enter the conclave for the election of the successor to Alexander VI. There are also many, many other eulogies. (Vol. II)

Perhaps the most notable eulogy was made a few years after the death of Alexander VI by an admirer of his, Egidius of Viterbo, who said:

...he had a most penetrating intelligence, was ingenious, prudent, industrious and had a natural eloquence apt to convince. No man ever acted more carefully,[11] persuaded more powerfully, defended more tenaciously. So great did he appear in all things that, in thinking, in speaking, in suffering, he would have been a great prince had not the qualities that adorned him been free and not eclipsed by many faults.[12] It would seem that nothing

---

[11] This habit of acting carefully would hardly fit with the other habit—attributed to him by his enemies—of openly acknowledging his illegitimate children!

[12] This last sentence, in De Roo's judgement, was merely a concession to the hatred and prejudice of the aristocracy which by then had become

prevented anyone who observed him publicly at work from asserting that he was born to command. He was very frugal of food and sleep, though fond of pleasures, although he never omitted on their account to perform public duties or to admit visitors; and he never refused his presence or his answer to any official caller. In spite of his kindness and activity, the time in which he lived was a sad, corrupt and disturbed period. (Vol. II)

During his life, Alexander VI had received many a token of appreciation and esteem from the people of Rome and from the Pontifical States, from colleagues, cardinals and popes under whom he had served. Extraordinary praises were bestowed on him in acknowledgement of his talents and virtues by Catholic princes who congratulated him through envoys, and also by some contemporary historians. In addition, the common people who opened their gates to his armies gave him a splendid reception whenever he paid visits and were tenaciously faithful to the Governments he had given them.

But his death put an end to all worldly praise of him. It was a triumph for the depraved nobility of the Pontifical States and for his enemies, ushering in a period of hatred and revenge.

---

dominant—it is noteworthy that, whatever faults may have been in the author's mind, not one of them was named.

CHAPTER 9

THE OTHER BORGIAS

The reputations of Cesar and Lucretia are hardly less vile than that of Rodrigo. The relevant facts about them are as follows.

Cesar abandoned considerable wealth when he gave up his clerical status in order to marry.[13] To do so he had, of course, to resign all his benefices. It is clear that he had never been happy in clerical life.

Lucretia was very virtuous. Contemporaries tell how she assisted sufferers, pawned jewels to help the poor, established religious institutions and hospitals, and from the age of 30 dressed simply and modestly. She had no ignominious past. The poet Ariosto praises her beauty, intelligence, works of piety and, above all, her chastity. She had children by two husbands. (Vol. I)

---

[13] A Pope has the power to dispense a cleric from his vows (indeed the power to dispense anyone from any vow) and the undoubted right to do so if he thinks it to be for the good of the cleric's soul. The Biblical text confirming that this authority exists is Matthew 16:18,19, "Thou art Peter, and upon this rock I will build My Church... And I will give to thee the keys to the Kingdom of Heaven. And whatsoever thou shalt bind upon earth, it shall be bound also in Heaven; and *whatsoever thou shalt loose upon earth, it shall be loosed also in Heaven.*"

Another "skeleton in the cupboard" of the Borgia family, according to almost universal belief, is Cardinal Francis de Borgia who is often falsely considered to be the illegitimate son of the exemplary pope, Calixtus III (Alphonsus de Borgia). However, no papal documents refer to a defect of legitimacy in his birth and he became a member of the Sacred College of Cardinals without any question arising. This would be completely impossible if he had been illegitimate. Illegitimacy is a canonical impediment to the reception of Holy Orders; and whereas dispensations from this impediment can be given (anyway for simple priests), the issue would have been bound to be raised and recorded. Francis de Borgia was in fact the son of Juan de Borja, the paternal uncle of Alexander VI.

CHAPTER 10

HOW CONCLUSIVE IS THE EVIDENCE, AND WHY?

L et us pause for a brief look at the evidence so far and see if we can decide whether it is conclusive.

Surely if there is one single piece of evidence that by itself would make nonsense of even the mildest of the allegations of shameless immorality against Alexander that are accepted without question by almost everyone but De Roo, it is the unanimity of Alexander VI's supposedly simoniacal election. It can be granted that it is possible to believe that some of the contemporary testimonies in favour of Alexander VI were made by parties who had a vested interest in flattering the current Vicar of Christ. It must also be granted, however, that it is equally possible to believe, given the open hostility of Julius II towards his predecessor Alexander, that many of the later testimonies hostile to Alexander were made by parties who had a vested interest in doing the reverse of flattering him, especially once he was in his grave; and that, as we shall see to be the case, it was under Julius that a caricature of Alexander that had no foundation began to obtain an undeserved degree of historical credit which was never refuted and which was accepted as at least partly reliable by later historians—even by those who found aspects of the legend puzzling. What is certain is that the two pictures of Alexander created by his contemporaries and near contemporaries—the one of a virtual saint and the other of a monster of vice—cannot both be true.

Nor is a compromise possible. Either one is true or the other.

The principal motive for rejecting the monster of vice in favour of the saint (I use the term loosely rather than in the sense of a man who has raised to the altar by the Church) is that, as will be shown in the next section, *all* of the evidence for the former is derived ultimately from parties who have no real claim to trustworthiness, and either obviously had, or could easily have had, ulterior motives for their deceit. By contrast, a considerable body of evidence in favour of the saint reaches us from unimpeachable authorities who went out of their way to bear witness to the Pontiff's goodness when such views were unpopular and against their own interests. Indeed we have grudging testimonies from Alexander's enemies. And of course there is the testimony provided by the unanimity of the conclave which elected him to the papacy.

What I now assert is that, since it is alleged that Alexander's immorality was open and well known, the cardinals could not have avoided knowing of it; and that, since they elected him unanimously as pope, the conclusion is inescapable that his alleged immorality was not open and well known and certainly did not include the flaunting of illegitimate children; and that in fact the unanimous election, even if it had not been followed by general approbation and rejoicing (which it was), proves beyond all doubt that Alexander was held to be the most fitting candidate for the papacy.

It must be stressed again that this unanimity, so rare in papal elections, leaves no room for a compromise view. It shows, of necessity, that every one of the cardinals believed that Rodrigo Borgia was the best suited of them all for the task of governing the Church; and only the most manifest of good men can earn such an accolade.

And of course it is for this reason that some historians, faced with this apparent contradiction to their picture of Alexander, have been moved to assert, with hopelessly inadequate evidence, that Alexander's election was simoniacal.

Is anyone put into doubt by the fact that the allegation of simony was first made by two cardinals, who however did so only after some considerable time had elapsed and then only by way of encouraging the King of France to depose Alexander? It is far less incredible that *two* cardinals should lie to serve their own ends than that *every* single cardinal should do so. Although it is an important theological and practical truth that sanctity wins enemies, it must not be forgotten that sinfulness does also. Even if Cardinal Borgia had the money to buy the votes of a large number of cardinals (which he had not), and even if the majority of the cardinals were his close friends and his partners in immorality with no concern for their souls (which they were not), are we to suppose that there was not a single cardinal who shrank from knowingly electing a figure of Satan himself to be the Vicar of Christ while swearing on the salvation of his soul that he had only the interests of the Church at heart? The impossibility is self-evident. And the only alternative to the ludicrous supposition that the conclave was bought is that the conclave elected a man so outstanding in virtue that no cardinal considered any other candidate more suitable.

And from the evidence just considered, it becomes clear that this single, indisputable circumstance of the unanimity of Alexandra's election is *in itself* sufficient to brand as beneath contempt even the slightest allegation of public immorality prior to the election, and thus to enable us to disregard in their entirety any other allegations deriving from the same sources.

CHAPTER 11

HOW AND WHY ALEXANDER VI'S SUBSEQUENT REPUTATION AROSE

A fter the death of Alexander VI, Pius III was unanimously elected. His name was Franciscus Piccolomini. He died after 25 days and was followed by Giuliano della Rovere who, like Alexander VI, was unanimously elected (barring his own vote) and became Julius II.

Alexander's death, as stated in the previous chapter, put an end to all worldly praise of him. According to Pastor, "when afterwards Julius II, the determined enemy of the Borgias, assumed the Government, it became usual to regard the 'Marrano', Alexander VI, as a pattern of all that is bad and wicked." Thus Msgr. De Roo informs us; and what he writes is confirmed by Michael Mallet (who, as already mentioned, is an author who by no means generally favours Alexander VI), in *The Borgias*:

> Alexander VI died surrounded by an atmosphere of hatred
> and fear; a hatred so violent that Julius II and all his successors
> refused to occupy the Borgia apartments in the Vatican, which
> were left neglected until the nineteenth century. It was this hatred
> which led the same Julius to torture confessions of crimes,
> supposedly committed at the command of the Borgias, out of
> Alexander's servants, and to eradicate as far as possible every
> evidence of Borgia achievement. Julius, as Cardinal Giuliano della

Rovere, had been Alexander's chief rival during his lifetime; first a rival in the papal election, and then the leader of those Cardinals who sought to depose him with French help. He had passed most of Alexander's pontificate in exile, stripped of many of his benefices, his boundless energy and ambition shackled by the success of his rival. It was Julius perhaps more than any other single person who set the tone of contemporary and later attitudes towards the Borgias.

But what Julius with his anti-Borgia activities had started, the humanist propagandists of the Italian princes and the local chroniclers of the cities of the Papal States completed. There are few of the contemporary observers and early sixteenth century commentators, whose reports and writings form the narrative sources for an account of the second Borgia pontificate, who can be described as entirely objective. Among the chroniclers, Stefano Infessura was a partisan of the Colonna and a violent anti-papalist whose writings did much to destroy the reputation of Sixtus IV as well as of Alexander. Matarazzo, the Perugian, was a client of the Baglione family and an opponent of papal government. Sigismondon de' Conti, a Curia official and therefore in sympathy with papal policies, was among the fairest reporters; but he was also a humanist historian to whom literary style and the introduction of apposite classical example were sometimes more important than factual accuracy. Then there were the Neapolitan publicists Sannazzaro and Pontano who poured out invective against the Pope who had abandoned their king to the mercy of foreign invaders. Ottaviano Ubaldini, who said of Alexander, 'Judas sold Christ for 30 denarii; this man would sell him for 29,' was a guardian of Guidobaldo da Montefeltro, Duke of Urbino, who was to be dispossessed by the Borgias. Guido Posthumus, another humanist critic, was employed by Giovanni Sforza, the divorced husband of Lucrezia Borgia and the author of charges of incest against her. There was the more influential Paolo Giovio, an employee of Orsini, Colonna and Medici patrons; Marin Sanuto, the Venetian diarist, into whose vast collection went every scrap of rumour and gossip about the Borgias whose policies caused so much alarm in Venice; and his fellow countryman, the diplomat Giustinian, who had learnt at first hand to distrust the Borgias, but admitted that it was easy to misinterpret their motives. Ambassadors, like Giustinian and his fellow Cataneo, the Mantuan, and Boccaccio, the Ferrarese, provide much of our information about Rome and the Borgias, but their reports were frequently flavoured by the political attitudes of the states which they represented and by their assessment of what their masters would like to hear.

High on the list of effective contemporary pamphlets comes the Savelli Letter, written anonymously for the benefit of Silvio Savelli, a Roman baron exiled by the Borgias. This was a tract, the extravagant invective of which made Alexander smile when it was read to him; but the echoes of its charges are to be found in many subsequent accounts. Another important source for the period is the diary of Johannes Burchard, the papal master of ceremonies. Burchard was a small-minded and prudish German, obsessed by his own failure to gain preferment, who gives us much valuable information on the daily life of the court, but who at the same time cannot be expected to have been either well-informed about Borgia policies or in sympathy with Borgia moral standards.

Finally, and most influential of all, came the Florentines, Niccolo Machiavelli and Francesco Guicciardini. Machiavelli's dispatches, although containing some of the most favourable contemporary descriptions of the Borgias, were often tinged with distortion designed to influence Florentine policy, and his later treatises have a polemical quality which at times twists the true facts. On the other hand Guicciardini, writing at a distance about events which he had often not witnessed at first hand, allowed his Florentine patriotism and his strong anticlericalism and anti-papalism to make his fine History a repository for some of the most virulent and least well authenticated of the Borgia legends.

Thus we see that, as De Roo asserts, those to whom we are chiefly indebted for making known Alexander's alleged crimes were never at any time in his presence.[14] (Vol. II)

Furthermore, there are many false documents in the archives of the Duke of Osuna in Madrid which have been used by those libelling Alexander VI. There is no record of them in the Vatican archives—this despite the fact that no authentic paper, whether diploma, Bull or brief, ever left the Roman Curia without being copied in the official registers.

It is a matter of historical record that many false Bulls were forged during the reign of Alexander VI. His secretary, Bartolomeo Florido, Archbishop of Cosenza, was, for instance, arrested in 1497 and found guilty of having forged over 3,000 false Bulls! He was condemned to death but the Pope commuted the sentence to life imprisonment. One example of a clear forgery is a purported Bull of Leo X attacking the morality of Alexander VI. Some patently false Bulls were also being slipped into the Vatican. Alexander VI in his Constitution *Cum Ad Sacrosancti* dated 1 April, 1503, states that falsifying Papal Bulls or briefs had been a reality in foregoing years. (Vol. I)

---

[14] For instance, Pontano, Sannazar and Guicciardini, who, says De Roo, produced their exposures in order to gratify the revengeful nobility of the Papal States and wrote entirely for mercenary reasons.

CHAPTER 12

BUT WHY?

Why was Alexander VI selected for libellous denigration and vilification that, as suggested earlier, are surely unequalled in history?

One clue is given by Margaret Monro on the first page of her 1943 book *Unlikely Saints*:[15]

> The Borgia Pope, Alexander VI, has been proved to be the victim of a whispering campaign, launched against him by the Roman nobility for the way he, a Spaniard, had curbed their not noticeably just ambition.

For further evidence I turn once more to Orestes Ferrara's *The Borgia Pope—Alexander the Sixth.*

> If no foreigner was especially esteemed by the Romans, the Catalans (as the Spaniards in Italy were then called) were literally hated... As in antiquity, the name of barbarians was given to all who were not the direct descendants of Rome...(and) Spain was regarded as an inferior nation even by comparison with the rest of

---

[15] To avoid any possible misunderstanding, I should mention that Margaret Monro does not include Pope Alexander VI among the saints referred to in the title of her book. She does, however, as she makes clear, realise that the allegations against him were fraudulent.

the barbarians, because it was the latest in date in the totality of countries of high civilization. (p.9)

This is a material factor, especially when it is remembered that (for excellent reason, as has been shown in Chapter 8) Alexander elevated nineteen Spaniards to the cardinalate during his pontificate and for the most part relied upon Spaniards as his advisors. It is not, however, sufficient in itself to account for the character assassination that took place, for his uncle, Pope Calixtus III, was equally Spanish and was tolerated to the extent of having become by our day almost entirely forgotten. The fundamental reason is that, as Ferrara describes next, Alexander VI acted without compromise as a statesman according to the dictates of his conscience and irrespective of the strength of the vested interests that the interests of the Church required him to trample on. On page 12 and following of Ferrara's book:

> The political programme of the new Pope was clearly shown from the very beginning. At Rome, the Pope must govern. Factions must disappear. The Pope does not need the help of powerful families, these families must not be powerful. Outside Rome, Alexander's view equally was that the Pope must govern the traditional possessions of the Church, even if he must use Vicars as intermediaries. The territories of Ravenna and the Pentapolis had been granted to the Sovereign Pontiff by Pepin the Short, after he had driven out the Lombards who had previously usurped them from the Roman Emperor in the East. If the Pope possessed of right these temporalities in the Romagna and elsewhere in central Italy, he must possess them in fact. If he did not effectively claim them, not only would he cease to fulfil his primary obligation to defend the Church, but he would

abandon whole populations who trusted him to the ferocity and rapine of such classical tyrants as the Bagliones, the Bentivoglios, the Malatestas, the Varanos and the rest. This idea was not new in Alexander VI. Certain previous Popes had thought likewise. They had even tried to put the thought into effect, but their strength was less than the strength of the usurpers. The so-called Vicars had occupied cities, territories and strongholds by violence, assassination, treachery and also through papal nepotism. Little by little, they had become independent of Rome. Bent only upon a life of luxury, they tyrannized over their peoples and bled them white. They were feudal lords, but by now they were a class of usurpers. They had once been necessary for war, but from that point of view they were now merely survivals of no practical value. They were organs which had ceased to be useful and hence had degenerated; and they continued to exercise their art, which was war, by selling their swords to the highest bidder, and making treason their principal source of income. Alexander decided from the beginning to destroy them the moment he had the strength for it.

So much for Rome. So much for the Papal States. For the rest of the world, Alexander wanted no invasions; he defended the status quo and aimed at such a balance of material power that the moral power of the papacy (though weakened by the new form of the national state and by the lessening of religious faith) might be decisive at least in the hour of great decisions if it could not be so continuously.

A programme of this sort maddened everybody. It ran counter to the designs of the kings of Europe, especially those of France and Spain who were in the process of founding a new all-conquering imperialism upon the ruins of the Holy Roman Empire. It collided with the designs of Venice, which was at that very moment ambitious of becoming a great power on the mainland since the Turk was driving it out of its maritime possessions. It collided with the designs of Naples, then under the rule of the insatiable King Ferrante, who meant to take Benevento and thus establish easy contact with the territory of Florence and be in a position to exercise an influence upon the north of Italy. But above all, Alexander's program threatened at the very foundation of their existence the great princely houses of Rome, and the still more numerous great houses of central Italy. For these families were the richest and most aggressive and had in their pay the best troops, the best poets and the best pamphleteers on the peninsula.

And he actually fought on two fronts, since he not only assailed the nobility but was determined to repress the excesses of the populace. He strictly maintained the law's authority over the lower classes. Though these lower classes were the objects of continual vexations, yet they had been allowed an evil latitude in the matter of obedience to the law, provided their breaking of the law did not damage the interest or caprice of the lord upon whom they depended. Alexander organized the administration of the city, expelled the men-at-arms who had come to sell themselves in this market of revolts, and vigorously prosecuted malefactors— who in all this moral confusion and absence of authority were protected by the victims themselves.

The Roman families fought against Alexander VI sword in hand with more or less success; but the combat they waged against him by false and dishonouring rumours was totally successful. To overcome him, they had to destroy his prestige, since his power lay principally in the prestige arising from his high office. The ancients crowned their victims with flowers before leading them to execution; but in an age when principles are abandoned, men cover their victims with mud.

Rome was in a ferment. Discontent against a government which insisted upon being a strong government gradually spread outwards from Rome to the rest of Italy and then over the Alps. The Pope's nepotism exposed an obvious flank for attack. And then began the great flood of: "it is said", "we hear", "everybody thinks". Diplomats, to satisfy the avidity of their governments for intrigue and their political interests, gathered up such rumours, even the feeblest.

The world reacted swiftly against Alexander's policy. The Orsini, the Colonna and other families now had a common enemy, so that we find them fighting on the same side, a thing unknown for centuries. King Ferrante of Naples, the incarnation of all abuses, a tyrant utterly vile and corrupt, turned into a moralist when the Pope checked his advance against the Papal States; and he wrote a letter for the Spanish sovereigns, which was the first calumnious document, denouncing the Pope's private life. To discredit the Pope, the Venetians united with the lords of the Romagna who were tyrannizing over their country, and against all decent usage informed the king of France of the secret discussions they had with the court of Rome. The Florentines, peaceful merchants, looked with an unquiet eye upon a Pope who wished Rome strong in the temporal order and ruled a vast region by which their own State was completely surrounded; they made use of Savonarola to combat him. The kings of France designed to invade Italy and occupy the Kingdom of Naples and the Duchy of Milan, and only the Pope was in their way. The King of Spain wanted to have a subordinate in Rome in the person of this Spaniard, while in Rome the Spaniard in question had precisely the opposite view. In the sphere of action, Alexander VI strove with consummate skill against all these difficulties; but in the sphere of opinion, against whispered slander and the calumny of anonymous pamphlets, he did not bother to make any reply at all.

It is a weakness that sometimes goes with greatness to believe that a cause can defend itself by its own justice.[16] Thus it was that there began that process of accusation in which only evidence adverse to him was held valid.

As De Roo's evidence has shown, Ferrara exaggerates somewhat the extent to which Alexander VI was calumniated during his own lifetime, but in substance what he says is clearly true and evidently shows sufficiently why the legend arose. That the legend should be maintained and built on as forcefully and enthusiastically as has since been the case is even easier to explain. The constant enemies of the Church have every reason to encourage public execration of a man who was a great statesman, a great religious reformer, a great promoter of public and private piety, and a person of uncompromising integrity and courage. And of course they gain the additional advantage of causing immeasurable damage to the Catholic Church by—on the deplorable admission of some of her most prominent historians—

---

[16] If weakness this be, it is a weakness that most of us would do well to acquire. Christ Himself, in the Beatitudes, said: "Blessed are ye when they shall revile you, and persecute you, and speak all that is evil against you, untruly, for my sake: Be glad and rejoice, for your reward is very great in heaven. For so they persecuted the prophets that were before you." (Matthew 5:11,12) I do not seek to imply, however, that Pope Alexander VI should not have taken whatever legitimate steps were available to him in order to defend himself against any slanders and libels that were circulating during his tenure of Church office. As individuals we may be glad to be unjustifiably reviled and abused, but a Pope is responsible also for the esteem with which his office is held and must therefore forego the luxury of ignoring attacks.

associating activities of barbarity, scarcely paralleled even among the most degenerate and licentious pagans, with the very Vicar of Christ Himself.